MAPS and EXPLORATION

Gareth Stevens
Publishing

Please visit our Web site www.garethstevens.com. For a free color catalog of all our high-quality books, call toll free 1-800-542-2595 or fax 1-877-542-2596.

Library of Congress Cataloging-in-Publication Data
Maps and exploration / Tim Cooke, editor.
      p. cm. -- (Understanding maps of our world)
   Includes index.
   ISBN 978-1-4339-3512-1 (library binding) -- ISBN 978-1-4339-3513-8 (pbk.)
   ISBN 978-1-4339-3514-5 (6-pack)
   1. Cartography--History--Juvenile literature. 2. Explorers--History--Juvenile literature.
   3. Voyages and travels--Juvenile literature. I. Cooke, Tim (Tim A.)
  GA105.6.M39 2010
  912.09--dc22   2009039219

Published in 2010 by
Gareth Stevens Publishing
111 East 14th Street, Suite 349
New York, NY 10003

© 2010 The Brown Reference Group Ltd.

For Gareth Stevens Publishing:
Art Direction: Haley Harasymiw
Editorial Direction: Kerri O'Donnell

For The Brown Reference Group Ltd:
Editorial Director: Lindsey Lowe
Managing Editor: Tim Cooke
Children's Publisher: Anne O'Daly
Design Manager: David Poole
Designer: Simon Morse
Production Director: Alastair Gourlay
Picture Manager: Sophie Mortimer
Picture Researcher: Clare Newman

Picture Credits:
Front Cover: Corbis: C.C. Shirley br; DigitalVision
9 - 10
Brown Reference Group: all artwork

Corbis: Bettmann12/13, 37; DigitalVision: 4m, 4b, 15, 17, 42; iStock: Agri Vision 34; Classix 22; El Flacode Norte 35; Eric Foltz 36; Pillon 29; Whitemay 31; Jupiter Images: Ablestock 5m, 20, 21, 23; Photos.com 8, 16, 33t, 33b, 38; Stockxpert 5t, 19, 25; Library of Congress: 24; Shutterstock: Eric Geveart 41; Gabriela Insuratelu Gianina 7; Jason Maehl 28; J. Matzick 40; Megastocker 44; Ricardo Manuel Silva De Sousa 9; Alex Vadinska 37; Steven Wright 5b

Publisher's note to educators and parents: Our editors have carefully reviewed the Web sites that appear on p. 46 to ensure that they are suitable for students. Many Web sites change frequently, however, and we cannot guarantee that a site's future contents will continue to meet our high standards of quality and educational value. Be advised that students should be closely supervised whenever they access the Internet.

Manufactured in the United States of America
1 2 3 4 5 6 7 8 9   12 11 10

CPSIA compliance information: Batch #BRW0102GS: For further information contact Gareth Stevens, New York, New York at 1-800-542-2595.

Contents

The Changing Shape of the World

1400

This map shows the world known to Europeans in the fifteenth century: Europe and parts of Asia and Africa.

1700

1600

In this seventeenth-century map, only the interior of North America and the southern oceans remain empty.

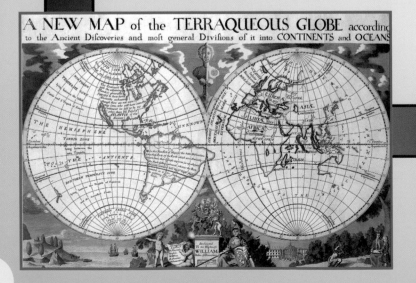

1800

This map reveals more information about Australia, but the northwest coast of North America and most of the Pacific Ocean remain unknown.

This sixteenth-century map fills in the coasts of Africa and India, the Caribbean islands, and parts of South America.

1500

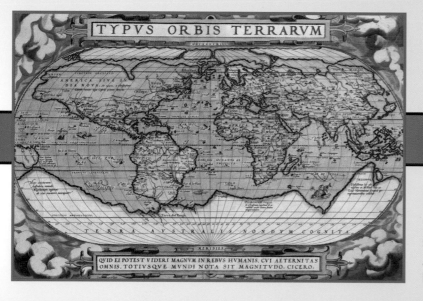

In this sixteenth-century map, South America is only roughly shaped; the northwest coast of Australia has become part of the legendary "southern continent."

The first photographs of Earth from space were taken in the 1960s.

1900

This world map was drawn in 1875, when Europeans were at the height of claiming colonies in other lands.

Introduction

This is a volume from the set Understanding Maps of Our World. This book looks at the link between mapmaking and exploration.

UNDERSTANDING MAPS OF OUR WORLD IS AN eight-volume set that describes the history of cartography, discusses its importance in different cultures, and explains how it is done. Cartography is the technique of compiling information for, and then drawing, maps or charts. Each volume in the set examines a particular aspect of mapping and uses numerous artworks and photographs to help the reader understand the sometimes complex themes.

After all, cartography is both a science and an art. It has existed since before words were written down and today uses the most up-to-date computer technology and imaging systems. Advances in mapmaking through history have been closely involved with wider advances in science and technology. Studying maps demands some understanding of math and at the same time an appreciation of visual creativity. Such a subject is bound to get a little complex at times!

About this Book

Many advances in mapmaking have been the result of exploration and colonization. Until the fifteenth century, practically half the world—the Americas and the Pacific Ocean—was unknown, and other vast areas such as the interior of Africa were very poorly mapped. European explorers made maps once they arrived. Gradually, the whole map of the world was filled in and made more accurate. There are now no places left on Earth that are unmapped. The rush to colonize new territories inevitably led to conflicts. One important role of colonial maps was to make sure that boundaries between countries and between neighbors were agreed on.

> ⊙ **The magnetic compass was invented in China in the first century A.D. It appeared in Europe in the twelfth century and was later vital in the Age of Discovery, when Europeans sailed around the world.**

Mapping Exploration

During the age of European discovery (about 1450–1900), exploration and mapmaking went hand in hand. As new discoveries were made, they were literally put on the map.

THE LANDS DISCOVERED BY THESE EXPLORERS WERE unknown to the West—but not to everyone. There were people living almost everywhere on Earth long before they were found by Europeans. These native peoples had their own maps, drawn on bark or animal hide, or painted as dots on rocks.

The explorers gave mountains and rivers European names and mapped the features that might be useful, such as the location of good harbors, land for farming, and mineral reserves. Ultimately, Europeans would use their maps to control the peoples of the lands they "discovered."

Thirteenth-century Arab nomads cross a desert on camels. Travelers around the world used different means to find their way.

A New Interest in Geography

The years from 1490 to 1510 saw enormous advances in mapmaking. At the same time, great voyages of discovery were being made by Columbus and others (see pages 10–13). Why did Europeans become explorers at this time?

One reason was the rediscovery of the works of the Greek geographer Ptolemy, who lived in the second century A.D. The Greeks knew that Earth was a sphere. They also knew about the geography of the Mediterranean, much of Asia and Europe, and parts of Africa. In order to record this knowledge, Ptolemy developed a way of representing the curved surface of Earth as a flat image. This was the first example of a map projection.

Ptolemy's *Geography* was rediscovered in 1410. The book sparked speculation about other lands. At the same time, there was great demand in Europe for luxury goods from the East, particularly spices from Southeast Asia. Long-distance trade was controlled by the Islamic nations of the Middle East, so European traders wanted to find alternative sea routes to the lucrative goods of the East.

In 1418, a Portuguese prince, Henry the Navigator, set up a school of navigation. The school brought together navigators, cartographers, and ship designers. The development of the caravel and the carrack, both ocean-going sailing ships, allowed them to sail down the western coast of Africa and eventually into the Indian Ocean.

The age of exploration was made possible by advances in ship design. Explorers often used caravels to explore the coastlines of the New World and larger ships like the carrack (pictured below) to carry supplies for the ocean crossing.

Encountering New Worlds

During the fifteenth and sixteenth centuries, countless expeditions were sent into the unknown. The information brought back meant maps were constantly being redrawn.

INSPIRED BY HENRY THE NAVIGATOR AND HIS SCHOOL of navigation, the Portuguese led the way in global exploration. By 1444, they had organized successful expeditions into the Atlantic Ocean. They sailed as far as Madeira, the Azores, and the Cape Verde Islands. Gradually, they began to travel further south along the west coast of Africa. As they did so, they left stone columns, marked with the date, to show where they had been. They founded trading forts along the coast, but had little interest in exploring inland.

In 1488, the Portuguese sailor Bartholomew Diaz was blown by storms all the way around the Cape of Good Hope—the southernmost point of Africa— showing there was a sea route into the Indian Ocean. In 1497, Vasco da Gama led a fleet of

→ **The major exploring nations were the Spaniards and the Portuguese. Although they claimed new lands as their own, they encountered indigenous groups of people everywhere they went.**

Arctic marine mammal hunters

sub-Arctic forest hunter-gatherers

Aleuts

plateau fishers and hunter-gatherers

west coast foraging, hunting and fishing peoples

remnant bison hunters

plains farmers

desert hunter-gatherers

Pueblo farmers

Mississippian temple-mound builders

Ir w fa

Hawaiian Islands

Bahamas

Cortés, 1519–25

Cuba

Jamaica

Hispaniola

Colu Co

Saavedra, 1527–28

North Andean chiefdoms

Amazonian chiefdoms

Arawakan manioc fa

Polynesians

Magellan, 1520–21

INCA EMPIRE

savanna hunter-ga

pampas hunter-ga

shellfish gatherers marine mammal hunters

three ships around the cape and across the Indian Ocean. He reached Calicut on the coast of India before returning to Portugal in 1499. In 1500, Pedro Cabral set sail from Lisbon to the cape on his way to India, but was taken by currents across the Atlantic to the then unknown coast of Brazil.

Only eight years earlier, Columbus had made the first of his four transatlantic voyages. His expeditions produced maps of the coastlines of islands such as Cuba and Hispaniola. As news of Columbus's discoveries spread, other European seafarers ventured across the Atlantic in search of fame and gold. Amerigo Vespucci, an Italian, sailed in a Spanish expedition to the mouth of the Amazon River in 1499, and in a Portuguese voyage along most of the Brazilian and

Argentine coasts in 1501. Vespucci was a good navigator and was able to accurately figure out the position of his ship. The information he brought back enabled European cartographers like the German Martin Waldseemuller (1480–1521) to update Ptolemy's world map. They added details of the recent discoveries made by Columbus and others. Waldseemuller's world map of 1507 was the first to mention the name "America" in honor of Amerigo Vespucci.

The Northerly Route

By now, other European countries were eager to make discoveries of their own. John Cabot, originally from Venice, set out from the English port of Bristol in 1497. Like Columbus, he was looking for a route to Asia. Cabot made landfall in Nova Scotia. He also explored along the coast of Labrador and Newfoundland. At the same time, he made many observations of the natural environment. Juan de la Cosa, Columbus's mapmaker, had access to Cabot's charts of the Canadian coast when producing his world map in 1500.

Cabot brought back news of rich fishing grounds off the coast of Newfoundland, and by 1500 it is thought that fishermen from Brittany, in northwest France, were regularly fishing there. In 1523, Jean Verazan (or Giovanni Verrazzano), an Italian living in France, sailed the length of the Atlantic coast from Florida to Newfoundland and claimed the whole area for the French king, Francis I. He described what is now New York Bay, and the sea passage into New York harbor is named for him.

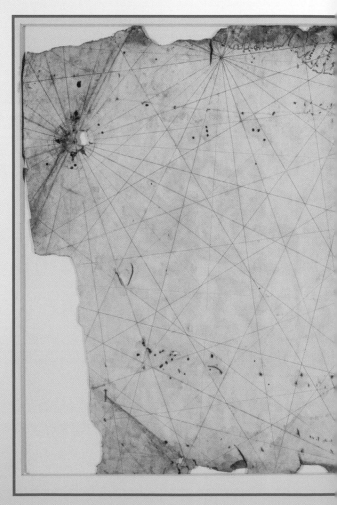

The most famous French explorer of the New World was Jacques Cartier. His three journeys to Canada—in 1534, 1535, and 1541—opened up the St. Lawrence River and provided a new route into the heart of North America.

Secret Information

European traders had been using coastal charts, known as portolans, for some time. They showed the locations of harbors, sandbanks, and dangerous rocks. As trading expeditions made longer and longer journeys away from Europe, demand grew for accurate sea charts. Trading countries made great efforts to keep all knowledge about their voyages secret, but sometimes their portolans were stolen by rivals. Others were captured by pirates.

DE RICCI NO. 151

SKELTON NO. 9

Juan de la Cosa accompanied Christopher Columbus as mapmaker on his second voyage to the Caribbean. On this chart of the New World, which was drawn on an ox hide in 1500, de la Cosa has named many places on the eastern coast, but nothing is mapped inland. Cuba is shown as an island, although Columbus had earlier made his crew swear that it was part of the mainland to reinforce his claims to have reached the coast of Asia.

Two Mapping Masters

People were eager to learn about the many New World discoveries, so the market for maps grew. This interest contributed to the development of cartography.

TWO INDIVIDUALS ABOVE ALL HELPED SHAPE THE NEW art of cartography: Gerardus Mercator (1512–1594) and Abraham Ortelius (1527–1598). Both were born in Antwerp, a city in what is now Belgium but was then part of the Spanish Netherlands. A busy commercial port, Antwerp was the most prosperous city in Europe at this time.

Gerardus Mercator

Mercator was originally a land surveyor. He helped produce an accurate map of Flanders (the area around Antwerp) in 1540. His interest in the methods of land surveying led him to spend some time as an instrument maker. A Protestant, Mercator was driven into exile in Germany in 1552 because of his religious beliefs. However, the international nature of mapmaking at this time meant that his work was still available to all.

Mercator was interested in Ptolemy's *Geography* and particularly his map projection (see page 9). He devised his own projection as an aid to navigation. Mercator's projection (see page 39) made it possible for a sea captain plotting a route to draw a bearing (a direction) on a map or chart using a straight line. First published in 1568, it quickly became extremely popular and is still widely used today. There is a good chance you will find the words "Mercator projection" printed in the margin of many topographic maps.

Mercator set up his own map-publishing business. The term "atlas," used for a collection of maps, was first used to describe a volume of maps of northern Europe published a year after his death.

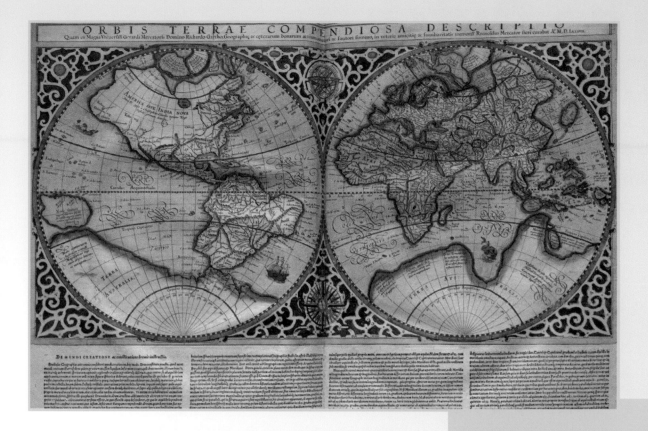

Abraham Ortelius

Although the term "atlas" belongs to Mercator, it was his younger contemporary, Abraham Ortelius, who first made a success of publishing map collections of this kind. At this time, maps were very large. Ortelius decided that maps would be easier to use if they were bound together as a book. The new atlases Ortelius designed took up less space and did not have to be folded or rolled up. His first atlas, called *Orbis Terrarum Theatrum (Theater of the World)*, was published in 1570. It contained 53 maps depicting all of the known world. Ortelius made use of information brought back by explorers, and names 87 cartographers whose work he consulted for the first edition. He praised Mercator as a "prince of modern geography."

Ortelius made the key decision to use consistent symbols to represent features such as towns, mountains, and forests. This is still done in all modern atlases.

⬆ Mercator's *Orbis Terrae Compendiosa (Comprehensive Map of the Lands of the Globe)*, which was produced in 1587. Mercator's map-publishing business was continued after his death by his son Rumold. Mercator's maps were still being published more than 70 years later.

The Dutch Golden Age

The period from 1570 to 1670 is known as the "Golden Age" in the Netherlands. Trade, commerce, art, and culture flourished, as did cartography.

THE VIBRANT ECONOMY OF THE NETHERLANDS MEANT that there was an increase in middle-class people who wanted to live comfortable lives in well-furnished homes. The rich burghers of Amsterdam and Antwerp developed a taste for decorative maps, such as those produced by Mercator and Ortelius.

Keeping Up with Demand

Skilled map engravers and printers set up businesses in cities such as Amsterdam and Antwerp to meet the increased demand for printed maps. They produced maps of all kinds: of local towns, of the whole country, of the new colonies, and of the entire world.

Both Mercator and Ortelius ran successful map-publishing businesses, but the most successful of all was that founded by Willem Blaeu (1571–1638). Blaeu had a specialized line in

One of Jan Vermeer's most famous paintings, *The Music Lesson*, shows a typical scene in a Dutch house of the seventeenth century. Many of Vermeer's interiors feature maps hanging on the walls.

16

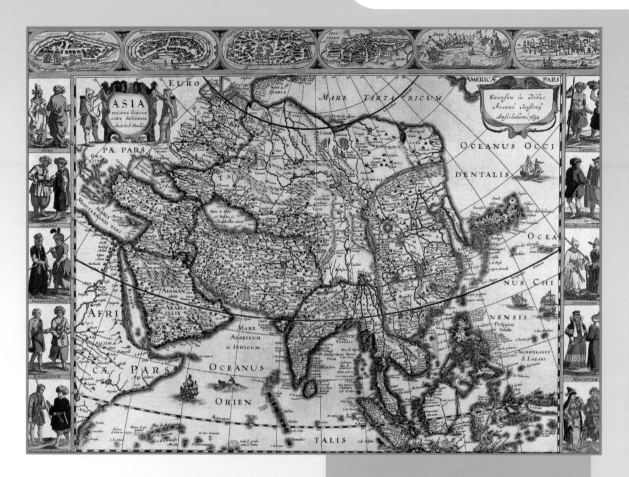

Willem Blaeu's 1640 map of Asia. The border is filled with attractive images of the exotic places shown on the map— portraits of native peoples and foreign traders with a series of bird's-eye views of cities and forts along the top. Such details gave his maps great appeal.

producing map globes. He was the official mapmaker to the Dutch East India Company and was able to add their new discoveries to his maps to keep them up-to-date. Sometimes wealthy people would ask Blaeu to create an atlas especially for them. The company Willem founded remained in business until 1700, run first by his son, and then by his grandson.

The expensive atlases of Dutch cartographers were eagerly bought by the prosperous, educated people of the Netherlands. They were sold in the city-center bookshops of Amsterdam, Delft, and Haarlem. Dutch mapmakers also exported their skills to other countries like Britain, France, and Germany. All the European nations relied on Dutch cartographers for their knowledge of the world.

Claiming Territory

The early European explorers were intent on colonization. As soon as they landed, they planted their national flag and claimed the place as a new possession.

ANY NATIVE PEOPLE WHO OBSERVED THIS CEREMONIAL claim being made would probably have been completely mystified by what was going on. The concept of "owning" a piece of land would very likely have been completely unfamiliar to them. Land belonged to the whole community, to their ancestors, or to the gods. The idea that unknown people could come from far away and claim it for themselves would have seemed nonsensical. On those occasions when Native American tribes "sold" the land to colonists for a few small gifts, no doubt they sometimes saw it as the best deal you ever could make—to sell something that nobody could own.

Agreements made with native peoples over the ownership ("title") of land were usually on very unequal terms. Native leaders could not read the words they were written in, and interpreters misled them about the nature of what they were agreeing to. Sometimes the colonizers did not even bother with treaties. They regarded the lands they claimed as *terra nullius* ("empty land") and the people already living there as having no rights of their own.

The Dutch colony of New Amsterdam on Manhattan Island in the seventeenth century. The Dutch "bought" Manhattan from local Native Americans for goods worth about $1,000 in modern value. New Amsterdam later passed to the British, who renamed it New York.

Nieuw-Amsterdam onlangs Nieuw jorck genomt. ende hernomen bij de Nederlanders op den 24 Aug: 1673. eindelijk aan de Engelse weder afgestaen

Making and Defending Claims

The European colonizers played things by their own rules. Nations like Spain, Portugal, Britain, France, and the Netherlands were in competition with each other to create overseas empires. They needed some way of showing who had claimed a particular piece of land. Keeping a flag flying on the beach was not practical, so they built forts and settlements, made maps of the new territory, and claimed the land "on paper."

As new lands were discovered and new colonies were founded or changed hands, maps of the world were constantly having to be amended or updated. One space, however, still remained marked as *terra incognita* (unknown land) on the world map—the "Great Southern Continent" that geographers believed lay in the southern hemisphere. It does exist, and is known today as Australia.

In the seventeenth century, Dutch and English sailors came close, but just missed sighting the continent itself. Then, in the mid-eighteenth century, when Britain and France were at war with each other over their colonies, both countries sent rival colonizing expeditions to the Pacific. As a result, Tahiti was claimed for France, and New Zealand and Australia for Britain.

Wineglass Bay in Tasmania was named by Europeans using a term no native Tasmanians would have recognized. Both the Dutch and the British charted the island, but it ended up in British control.

Colonial Mapping

Once a claim had been made, one of the first tasks was to set about making detailed maps of the colony. This was another equally important way of taking possession.

MAPMAKING USUALLY STARTED BEFORE A LANDING had been made—coastlines could be charted by making accurate observations from ships close to shore. Soundings, or depth readings, would be taken of coastal and estuarial waters to find navigable seaways for ships and plan the sites of harbors.

Knowing the shape of the land was important. The selection of good sites to build defensive stockades and forts to protect their new settlements—on high ground or near a harbor, for example—relied on detailed mapping.

⬇ **An eighteenth-century map of Jamaica and Barbados. The information shown includes major settlements and an indication of mountainous terrain.**

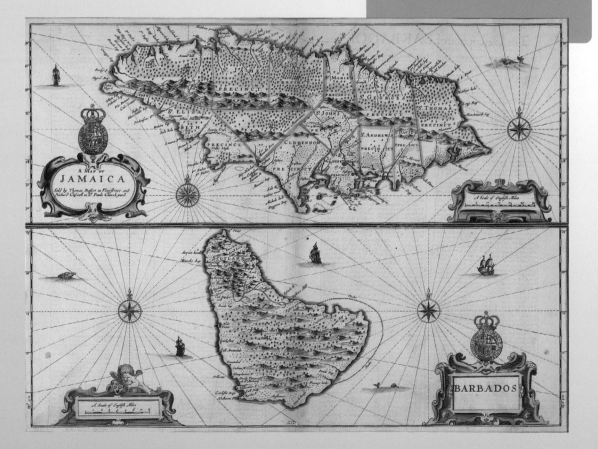

Once the protecting forts were built, work could begin on planning and building a permanent settlement. The next stage was to send surveyors into the interior to document the colony's resources. Was there fertile land for farming where plantations could be established for coffee or sugar? Were there gold reserves for mining? As the "white spaces" on the maps were filled in, settlers began moving into the interior, and the maps were used as legal documents to decide the distribution of land. Native villages were marked on the map, confining the indigenous peoples to a particular area. This made it easier to control the local people and to exploit them as a source of labor.

This seventeenth-century map shows what is now Argentina and Peru. Although parts of the Parana River valley are populated, many parts of the map remain blank. European cartographers only recorded European settlements and other features that were useful to colonists rather than native people.

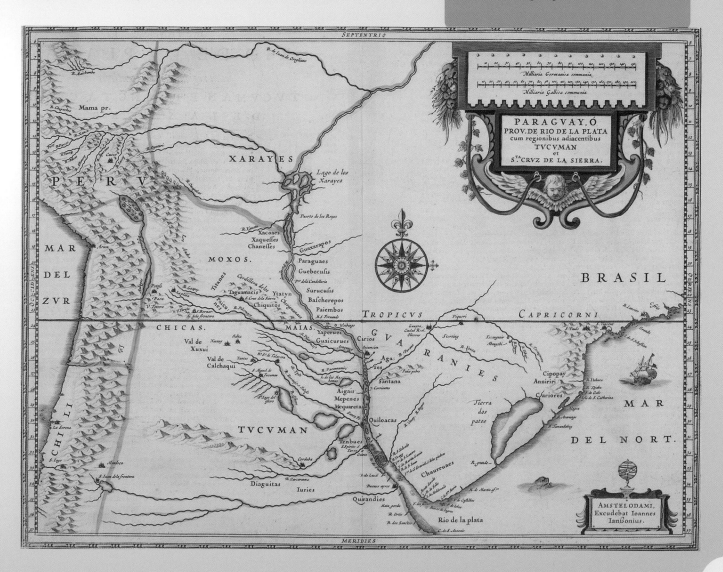

Early Maps of America

At first, North America did not seem to have much to offer Europeans. Early visitors reported that it was covered in thick forests and inhabited by hostile natives.

MANY EARLY ATTEMPTS AT COLONIZATION RAN INTO difficulties. German engraver Theodor de Bry drew the map of Florida shown below for a volume that he published in 1591. He based his map on early travelers' accounts, but his map is very inaccurate. For example, de Bry did not know that Fort Caroline had been destroyed by the Spanish 36 years earlier.

Familiar Landscapes

As the first settlers cleared forests for farmland, they created a European-looking landscape. They gave places familiar names from home, replacing the Native American names. This process can be

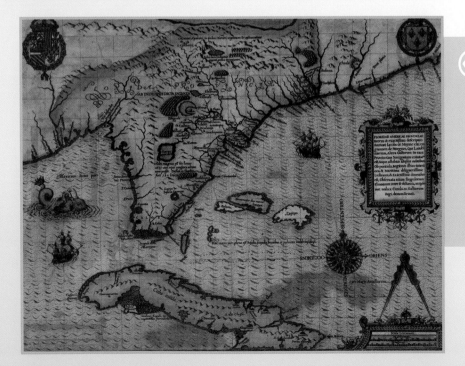

On Theodor de Bry's colonial map of 1591, the island of Cuba is more recognizable than the Florida coastline.

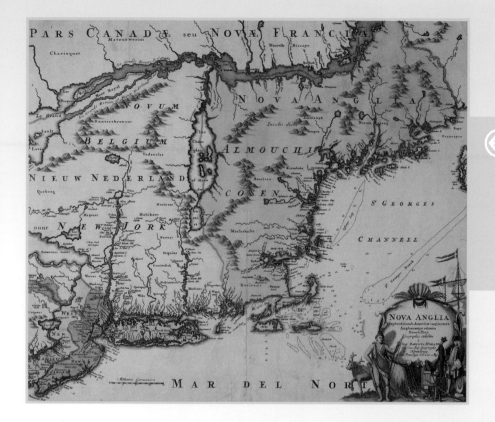

This map of New England was created in 1714. It uses different colors to distinguish New England from New Netherland to the west. To the north lies New France, which is labeled as being part of Canada.

seen on some of the very earliest colonial maps of North America created by Englishman John Smith (1580–1631), who founded Jamestown, Virginia, in 1607.

On Smith's map of New England (1616), the river that the local people knew as Massachusetts became the Charles River in honor of Smith's patron, the Prince of Wales (later King Charles I). Accomack became Plymouth, Sagoquas became Oxford, Aggowan became Southampton, and so on.

Colonial maps can tell us a lot about the way early settlements were organized. In French Canada, for example, land holdings took the form of long, thin strips of land that had a narrow river frontage and stretched back a long way into the forest. By contrast, field patterns in English parts of North America were much more compact. The Spanish in the Southwest divided up land into a regular grid pattern.

These were all habits brought from the Old World, another way of taming the wilderness by making it look more like home.

Crossing the Continents

By the late eighteenth century, explorers had traveled far up the Mississippi and Missouri River valleys, but none had found a route across the Rockies to the Pacific Ocean.

THE UNITED STATES WAS ONLY 27 YEARS OLD WHEN President Thomas Jefferson decided to purchase the Louisiana Territory from France. This territory covered an area of 828,800 square miles (2,147,000 sq km) in the South and Midwest. The "Louisiana Purchase" of 1803 doubled the size of the republic, ensured free navigation on the Mississippi River, and gave the United States control of a vast area of valuable land. Jefferson had long dreamed of discovering a land route to the Pacific Ocean, and had promoted three expeditions that failed to do so.

The 1810 map by William Clark shows the complete expedition, from St. Louis (bottom righthand corner) to the mouth of the Columbia River (top left). It is remarkable for its accurate depiction of the upper Missouri and the multiple ranges of the Rockies.

This postage stamp, issued to mark the 250th anniversary of the journey, shows Lewis and Clark with their Shoshone guide, Sacajawea. She was valuable guide for the crossing of the Rocky Mountains.

Even before the Louisiana Purchase was finalized, Jefferson was organizing a new expedition to set out along the Missouri River and into the Northwest. He chose his personal secretary, Meriwether Lewis, to lead the "Corps of Discovery," as it became known. Lewis was soon joined by William Clark, a soldier and frontiersman. The two men agreed to share the task of leading the expedition.

Lewis and Clark left Camp Dubois near St. Louis in May 1804 and traveled by boat up the Missouri River. Jefferson had instructed them to report on the geography, local peoples, plants, and animals of the regions they explored, so they kept a detailed journal.

By November, Lewis and Clark had reached the villages of the Mandan and Hidatsa peoples of North Dakota. Here they hired a French Canadian trapper, Toussaint Charbonneau, to act as an interpreter. His young Shoshone wife, Sacajawea, also joined the expedition. Sacajawea acted as a translator and sometimes as a guide. Her presence in the group also played an important role in persuading the Native American peoples they encountered that the expedition was friendly.

By December 17, it had grown too cold to continue, so they stopped at Fort Mandan. Here Clark produced detailed maps of their route before they set out again in April 1805.

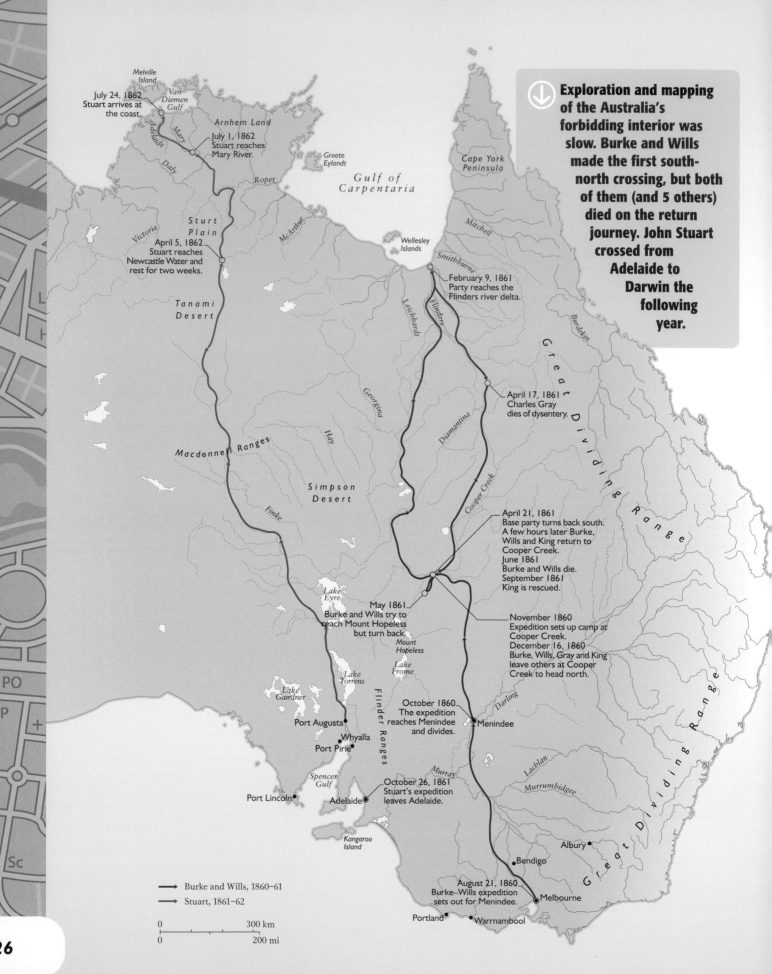

July 24, 1862
Stuart arrives at
the coast.

Melville
Island

Van
Diemen
Gulf

July 1, 1862
Stuart reaches
Mary River.

Arnhem Land

Groote
Eylandt

Gulf of
Carpentaria

Cape York
Peninsula

Exploration and mapping of the Australia's forbidding interior was slow. Burke and Wills made the first south-north crossing, but both of them (and 5 others) died on the return journey. John Stuart crossed from Adelaide to Darwin the following year.

Sturt
Plain

April 5, 1862
Stuart reaches
Newcastle Water and
rest for two weeks.

Victoria

Roper

McArthur

Smithburne

Wellesley
Islands

Mitchell

February 9, 1861
Party reaches the
Flinders river delta.

Flinders

Leichhardt

Burdekin

Tanami
Desert

Macdonnell Ranges

Georgina

Hay

Diamantina

April 17, 1861
Charles Gray
dies of dysentery.

Finke

Simpson
Desert

Cooper Creek

Great Dividing Range

April 21, 1861
Base party turns back south.
A few hours later Burke,
Wills and King return to
Cooper Creek.
June 1861
Burke and Wills die.
September 1861
King is rescued.

Lake
Eyre

May 1861
Burke and Wills try to
reach Mount Hopeless
but turn back.

Mount
Hopeless

November 1860
Expedition sets up camp at
Cooper Creek.
December 16, 1860
Burke, Wills, Gray and King
leave others at Cooper
Creek to head north.

Lake
Frome

Lake
Torrens

Lake
Gairdner

Flinder Ranges

October 1860
The expedition
reaches Menindee
and divides.

Darling

Menindee

Port Augusta

Whyalla
Port Pirie

Spencer
Gulf

Murray

Lachlan

Murrumbidgee

October 26, 1861
Stuart's expedition
leaves Adelaide.

Port Lincoln

Adelaide

Kangaroo
Island

Albury

Bendigo

Great Dividing Range

August 21, 1860
Burke–Wills expedition
sets out for Menindee.

Melbourne

Portland

Warrnambool

→ Burke and Wills, 1860–61

→ Stuart, 1861–62

0   300 km
0   200 mi

The group continued their journey up the headwaters of the Missouri River. Snow began to fall as they crossed the Rocky Mountains of Montana, but eventually they found the headwaters of the Columbia River system. By November, they had reached the Pacific coast of Oregon. They held a vote to decide where they should set up their winter camp and finished work on a small fort by December.

Their return journey was made in one season (March to September 1806). In total, the party had traveled nearly 8,000 miles (13,000 km) to confirm the claims of the United States to extensive land rights beyond the original Louisiana Territory.

Across Australia

More than half a century after the first overland route across North America was discovered, the vast continent of Australia was crossed for the first time.

The first settlers did not want to move away from the coastal settlement of Sydney, on the east coast. More land was needed for farming, however, so explorers sought and found a route across the Blue Mountains in the southeast corner. The area on the other side was the largest river basin in Australia. It was mapped and surveyed in 1828. The aborigines who occupied these lands were rounded up and slaughtered.

In 1861, Robert Burke and William Wills, a professional surveyor, set out to cross Australia from south to north. Their goal was to find an overland route to extend the telegraph cable from India. They completed the journey of more than 1,400 miles (2,250 km) from Adelaide to the Gulf of Carpentaria, but both died on the return journey. Only one of their companions survived. Less than a year later, John Stuart found a faster alternative route, which was chosen for the telegraph cable in 1872.

Mapping India

In the mid-eighteenth century, the Mughal Dynasty, which had ruled much of India for 200 years, was in decline. In 1758, the British East India Company took control of Bengal.

THE COMPANY ORDERED A CARTOGRAPHIC SURVEY of Bengal. In charge was James Rennell (1740–1830), the Surveyor General of Bengal. Rennell's *Atlas of Bengal*, published in 1779–81, became the starting point for all future mapmaking in India.

In 1799, Mysore came under British control. This meant more maps were needed, and Captain William Lambton began what became a huge surveying enterprise. In 1817, his assistant, George Everest (1790–1866), assumed responsibility for the Great Trigonomical Survey of India. It would take more than 60 years to complete the work.

⊕ **Mount Everest in the Himalayas is the highest point on Earth's crust. Modern measurements give its height as 29,029 feet (8,848 m).**

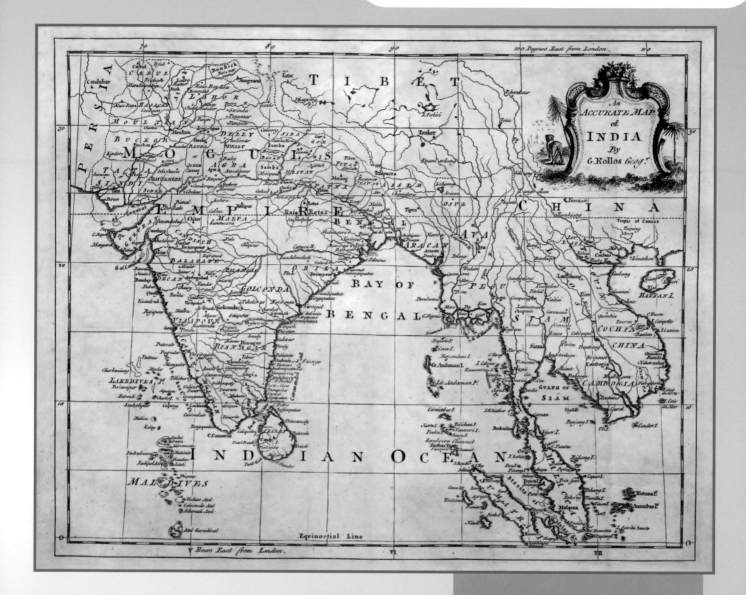

Everest had to overcome many problems. Cholera and malaria affected over 150 of his men, and ten died. The forests of the Ganges Valley made it difficult to take measurements of distant landmarks, so he had to build observation towers. The greatest undertaking of all was the mapping of the mighty Himalayas, the mountain range that divides India from Asia. After 15 years, the first detailed maps ever made of the Himalayas were produced. George Everest called all the peaks by their local names. After his retirement, the British directors of the survey broke with his policy and decided to name the highest peak Mount Everest.

Mapping India and other parts of Southeast Asia became more pressing for the British as their empire expanded to include more territory in the Subcontinent.

The Scramble for Africa

Only the coasts of Africa were mapped in accurate detail on European maps compiled between the fifteenth and eighteenth centuries.

THE LAND SOUTH OF THE SEEMINGLY IMPASSABLE Sahara desert was a mystery to Western mapmakers. The area beyond the Sahara was called the "Dark Continent." This was thought to be a fatally dangerous place for Europeans. It was the discovery of vast deposits of gold, silver, and copper that led to a rapid "opening up" of the interior of the continent.

The first accurate mapping of Africa began in the eighteenth century. French cartographers used reports from missionaries and traders to map Ethiopia in East Africa, for example. By the end of the century, serious exploration of Africa's great river systems got underway. In the nineteenth century, scientific bodies such as the Royal Geographical Society sponsored expeditions into the African interior to identify the headwaters of the Nile, the great river that flows for 4,160 miles (6,695 km) from Lake Tana in Ethiopia to the Mediterranean Sea.

One of those who looked for the river source was David Livingstone, the most

This map of Africa, drawn in the mid–nineteenth century, shows what Europeans knew about the continent at that time. While some regional states are shown in color, much of the African interior is still "empty" space with few details.

Map of Africa in 1914 with the country or colonial zone boundaries emphasized. France had claimed the most land during the previous 20 years, but much of its territory in West Africa covered the Sahara.

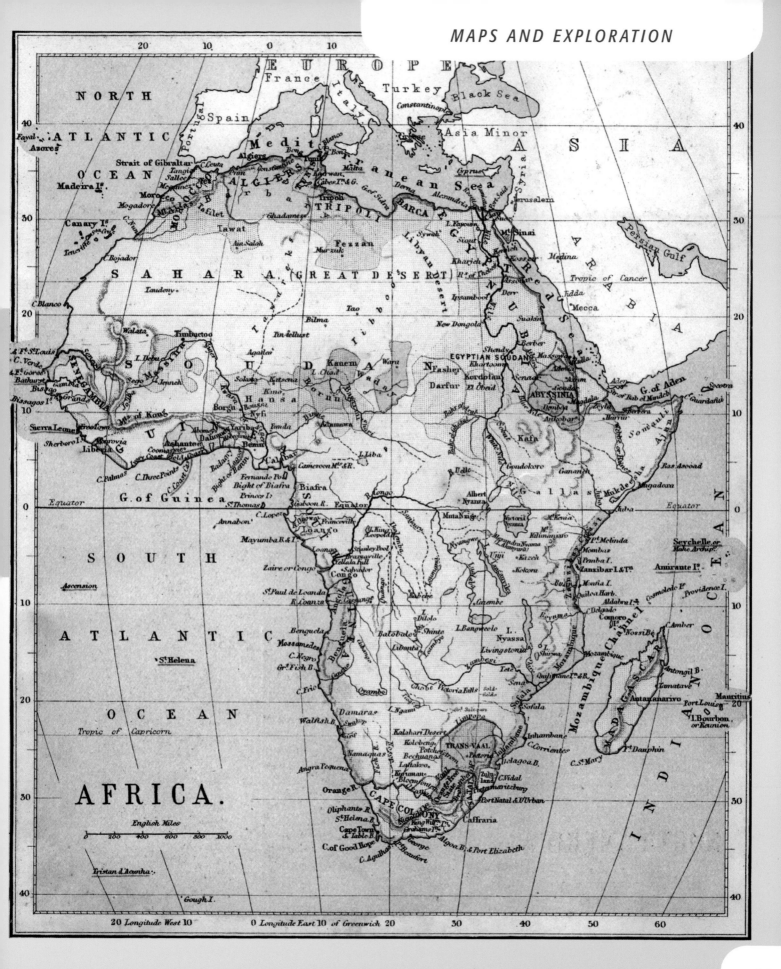

AFRICA.

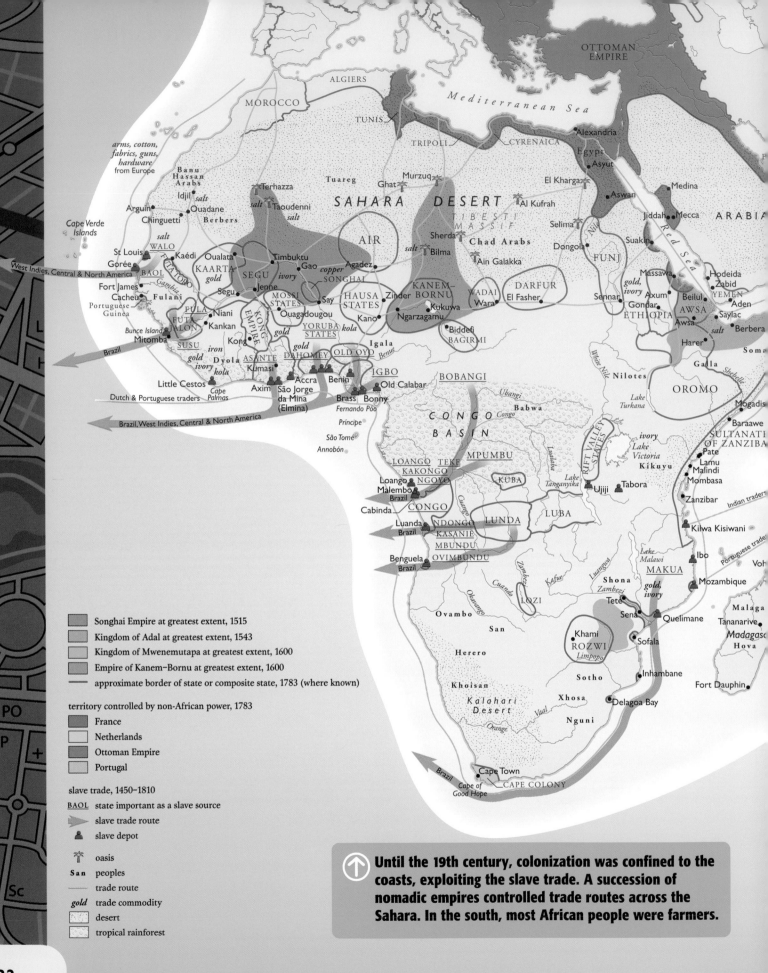

OTTOMAN
EMPIRE

ALGIERS

MOROCCO

Mediterranean Sea

TUNIS

TRIPOLI   CYRENAICA

Alexandria

Egypt
Asyut

*arms, cotton,
fabrics, guns,
hardware*
from Europe

Banu
Hassan
Arabs

Idjil *salt*

Terhazza

Murzuq

Ghat

SAHARA DESERT

El Kharga

Aswan

Medina

Jiddah Mecca

ARABIA

Arguin
Chinguetti   Ouadane
Berbers

salt Taoudenni
salt

salt

Al Kufrah

TIBESTI
MASSIF

AIR

Sherda

Selima

Dongola

FUNJ

Suakin

Cape Verde
Islands

salt

St Louis WALO
Gorée   Kaédi

WALO

Oualata
Timbuktu
Gao

Agadez
copper

salt Bilma

Chad Arabs

Ain Galakka

Massawa

Hodeida
Zabid

YEMEN

West Indies, Central & North America

BAOL

KAARTA
gold

SEGU
Segu
Jenne

ivory

SONGHAI

HAUSA
STATES
Kano

Zinder

KANEM–
BORNU
Kukuwa

Ngarzagamu

WADAI
Wara

DARFUR
El Fasher

Sennar

Axum
Gondar

ETHIOPIA

Awsa
AWSA

Aden

Saylac

Berbera

Fort James
Cacheu
Portuguese
Guinea

Fulani

MOSSI
STATES

Ouagadougou

Say

Biddefi
BAGIRMI

Harer

Soma

FUTA
TORO

FULA
FUTA
JALON

Niani
Kankan

Igala

KONG
EMPIRE

YORUBA
STATES
kola

OLD OYO
Benue

*gold,
ivory*

Bunce Island
Mitomba

SUSU

iron

Kong

gold

DAHOMEY

IGBO

BOBANGI

Nilotes

OROMO

Mogadis

Brazil

*gold
ivory*

Dyola
kola

ASANTE
Kumasi

gold

Benin

Old Calabar

Babwa

Lake
Turkana

Galla

Baraawe

Little Cestos
Dutch & Portuguese traders

Axim   São Jorge
da Mina
(Elmina)

Accra

Brass Bonny

Fernando Pôo

CONGO
BASIN

Ubangi

Congo

ivory
Lake
Victoria

Kikuyu

SULTANATE
OF ZANZIBAR
Pate
Lamu
Malindi

Cape
Palmas

Brazil, West Indies, Central & North America

São Tomé

Annobón

Principe

MPUMBU

Ujiji

Tabora

Mombasa

Indian traders

LOANGO
KAKONGO
Loango NGOYO
Malembo
Brazil

TEKE

KUBA

Lake
Tanganyika

Zanzibar

Cabinda

CONGO

NDONGO

LUNDA

LUBA

Kilwa Kisiwani

Portuguese traders

Luanda
Brazil

KASANJE
MBUNDU

Lake
Malawi

Ibo

Voh

Benguela
Brazil

OVIMBUNDU

MAKUA

*gold,
ivory*

Mozambique

Zambezi

Shona
Tetê

Luangwa

Kafue

LOZI

Cuando

Ovambo

San

Herero

Sena

Quelimane

Sofala

MALAGA

Tananarive

Madagasc

Hova

Khami
ROZWI
Limpopo

Okavango

Khoisan

Kalahari
Desert

Vaal

Orange

Sotho

Xhosa

Nguni

Inhambane

Fort Dauphin

Delagoa Bay

Cape Town
*Cape of
Good Hope*   CAPE COLONY

Brazil

Legend:

- Songhai Empire at greatest extent, 1515
- Kingdom of Adal at greatest extent, 1543
- Kingdom of Mwenemutapa at greatest extent, 1600
- Empire of Kanem–Bornu at greatest extent, 1600
- approximate border of state or composite state, 1783 (where known)

territory controlled by non-African power, 1783

- France
- Netherlands
- Ottoman Empire
- Portugal

slave trade, 1450–1810

- BAOL state important as a slave source
- slave trade route
- slave depot
- oasis
- **San** peoples
- trade route
- *gold* trade commodity
- desert
- tropical rainforest

↑ **Until the 19th century, colonization was confined to the coasts, exploiting the slave trade. A succession of nomadic empires controlled trade routes across the Sahara. In the south, most African people were farmers.**

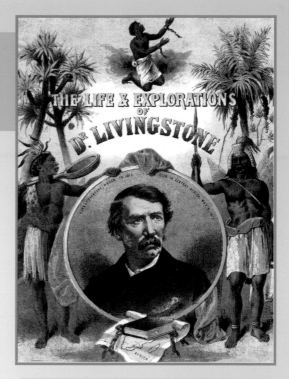

The exploits of missionary David Livingstone put Africa on the map for Victorians. His travels made him a British national hero.

famous African explorer of his day. A Scottish missionary, he undertook his long journeys through the heart of Africa in the hope of winning Christian converts and ending slavery.

Mineral Wealth

Until the late ninteenth century, Africa seemed empty of resources for Europeans to plunder. The largest, and most terrible, trade was in people. Some 10–15 million people were shipped as slaves across the Atlantic before the trade was largely ended in 1808. The trade in ivory and other commodities was mostly controlled by Arabs. Then, in 1871, diamonds were discovered at Kimberley in South Africa. This was soon followed by reports of other great mineral reserves: gold, copper, and coal. European countries rushed to stake out claims to vast areas of land and seize control of Africa's untapped wealth.

After Livingstone went missing for five years, he was found by the journalist Henry M. Stanley, a reporter with the *New York Herald* (below). Stanley greeted the explorer with the words, "Dr. Livingstone, I presume?"

A New Map of Africa

In 1884–85, a conference was held in Berlin, the capital of Germany, to settle rival European claims over parts of Africa (see map on page 31). A new map of Africa emerged as the known details of the landscape were recorded, and new boundaries drawn up allocating different parts of the continent to the colonizing powers.

Vital decisions were made on the basis of inaccurate, small-scale maps. Boundaries were imposed as straight lines across the landscape regardless of existing tribal boundaries or migration routes. Land was carved up to suit the needs of the colonizers. For Africa, the result has been a terrible history of war and conflict.

"Good Fences Make Good Neighbors"

Exploring, mapping, and settling new lands was soon followed by conflicts over who owned what territory. Maps themselves were often the cause of these disputes.

ONE NATION'S MAP MIGHT SHOW THE BOUNDARY OF their country in one place; the country next door might say that it was in the "wrong" place and that the piece of territory belonged to them. The inevitable result was armed conflict.

The Mexican-American War (1846–48), for example, was fought over the disputed territory of Texas between the Nuerces River and the Rio Grande, occupied by U.S. troops. The War of the Pacific (1879–84) saw Chile pitted against Peru and Bolivia for control of the nitrate-rich Atacama Desert, resulting in Bolivia losing its access to the ocean. To solve arguments of this kind, both countries must reach a legal settlement about the exact line of the international boundary.

A marker on the border between the Netherlands and Belgium. Does it really matter where the boundary lies? Now both countries are in the European Union, so it might be less important than before, but it may still matter—to loggers who work in the forest, for example.

↑ **This fence runs along the border between the United States and Mexico. The United States built it to keep out illegal immigrants.**

The American–Canadian Border

The longest undefended national boundary in the world, the American–Canadian border, extends 5,525 miles (8,890 km). Settlement of the line tested the goodwill of governments and the skill of judges and surveyors. Final agreement came only in the early twentieth century.

The section of the border between the Atlantic and the Great Lakes was first agreed upon in 1783. But the land had not been surveyed, and there were no accurate maps. An international boundary commission was set up in 1794 to resolve disputes, and in 1847, the eastern border was agreed. It divides Lakes Ontario, Erie, Huron, and Superior—important waterways for both nations.

There were significant disputes about the boundary between the Great Lakes and the Pacific before the 49th parallel (the line of latitude at 49°N) was fixed as the boundary in 1846. The ownership of islands in the Pacific was not resolved until 1873. In 1903, it was decided that the north-south border between Alaska and the Yukon Territory should run in a straight line along a line of

longitude. It took 10 years, from 1904 to 1914, to make a full survey of this frozen, mountainous terrain.

A permanent International Boundary Commission for the whole border was set up in 1925. Its main task is to ensure that the border is clearly marked. More than 8,000 reference monuments—usually piles of cemented stones or short pillars— define its route; the border itself is the straight-line segments that join these monuments across the landscape.

Defended Borders

In many other parts of the world, high barbed-wire fences and security chains mark borders, and armed checkpoints and watchtowers replace friendly border stones. In extreme cases, nations plant land mines along their border zones to stop invasion or sometimes to stop their own citizens from leaving.

Disputed borders cause problems for mapmakers. The Indian government allows no map to be published in India showing the disputed border of Kashmir, a disputed territory that is claimed by both Pakistan and India.

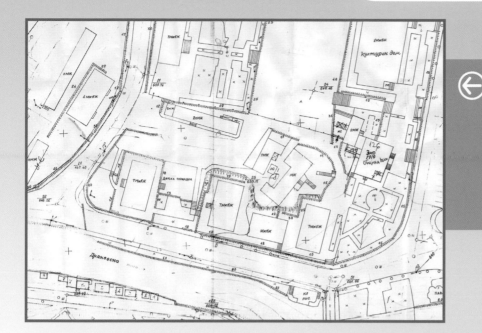

Here is an example of a computer-generated cadastral map with all the markers that define the property boundaries shown. The markers are usually nails, small pipes, or posts hammered into the ground at the corners of properties.

Property Boundaries

Land is valuable, and so the boundaries need to be agreed on the ground, recorded on a map, and accepted by the property owners. Cadastral maps show the exact location of property boundaries. They are among the earliest known uses of large-scale mapping. Many countries have now introduced computerized systems to record all their land boundaries.

A cadastral engineer from the U.S. General Land Office holds a couple of boundary markers prior to staking a claim in Antarctica in 1940. He is preparing to hammer them into the ice. The United States has since given up this claim.

Bias in Maps

There are very few colonies left in the world today—only a handful of islands in the Caribbean and the Pacific—but many maps still show what is known as colonial bias.

MAPS WITH A COLONIAL BIAS SHOWED FEATURES that reflected the values of the imperial power rather than those of the governed. More often than not, the symbols used were not suited to represent the very different landscapes of distant parts of the world. Agricultural and urban features in Kenya or Vietnam, for instance, were far from resembling those in Britain or in France, but the mapmakers did not show this. A cultivated field marked on a map of Australia, for example, was more likely to be a rough paddock for running livestock.

As colonies became independent countries, most of them wanted to discard all references to their colonial past.

Victoria Falls in Africa was named for Britain's queen. Local people called it Mosi-oa-Tunya ("the Smoke that Thunders").

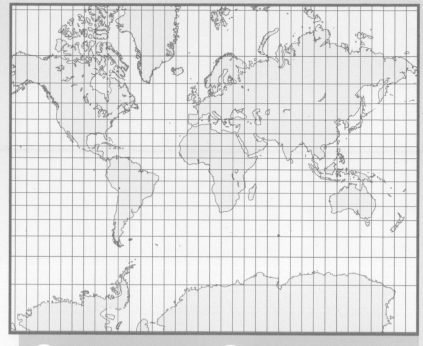

Explorers had named many features in the landscape after national figures or places back home. Britain's Queen Victoria, for example, had countless places across the globe named after her. Now these names were dropped, and ones more closely representing indigenous values were introduced. In Australia, for example, the great rock feature that Europeans named Ayers Rock has reverted to its aboriginal name of Uluru on modern maps.

New Views of the World

The traditional world map is centered on Europe, but there is no strong reason for this. A world map centered on the Pacific Ocean might have a lot of sea in the middle of it, but it would offer a more relevant view of the world for people in Indonesia and Peru than the traditional one.

Look at the two projections on the right. Europe looks much larger in relation to Africa on the Mercator projection than it does on the Peter's projection below it. Many people feel that the continued use of the Mercator projection reflects colonial bias, and that projections such as the Peter's give a better indication of the relative sizes of countries. Despite this, the Mercator projection still dominates world mapping.

Mercator's projection was developed in the sixteenth century as an aid to navigation. Mercator himself never produced a map of the whole world on this projection, and it is not really suitable for that purpose. Its major problem is that it exaggerates the size of areas close to the poles.

The Peter's projection shows each country with its correct area. This projection more accurately represents the relative sizes of the parts of the world that were colonized by European nations. The United Nations has adopted the Peter's projection for its world maps.

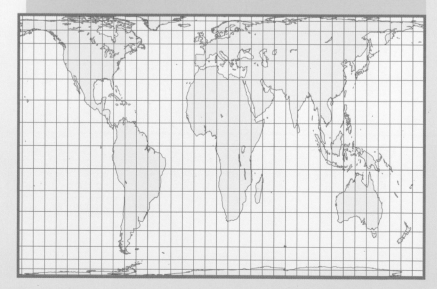

Glossary

Words in *italics* have their own entries in the glossary.

aborigines – the original inhabitants of an area, in particular the original inhabitants of Australia and their descendants. *See also* native peoples

agriculture – the cultivation of plants and the keeping of domestic animals to support human populations

altitude – height or vertical distance above mean sea level; or the degrees of elevation of a star, the sun, or the moon above the horizon

astronomy – the scientific study of celestial bodies (planets and stars) and of the universe as a whole. People who do this are called astronomers.

atlas – a collection of maps with a uniform design bound together as a book

bearing – the direction someone is heading measured as an angle away from north. Due north has a bearing of 0 degrees, while due west has a bearing of 270 degrees. Bearing is also sometimes used to describe angular position or direction in relation to any two known points.

burgher – a prominent citizen in a medieval European city, usually one who was on the town council or had considerable influence

cadastral system – a method of recording ownership of land based on registers, legal documents, and maps showing the boundaries of individual tracts

cartographer – someone who collects information and produces maps. The task of making maps is called cartography.

colonial America – the original 13 colonies of North America forming the United States

The effects of agriculture can be easily seen from the air. This aerial photograph shows the different crops being grown in an area, as well as the way that agricultural land is divided up.

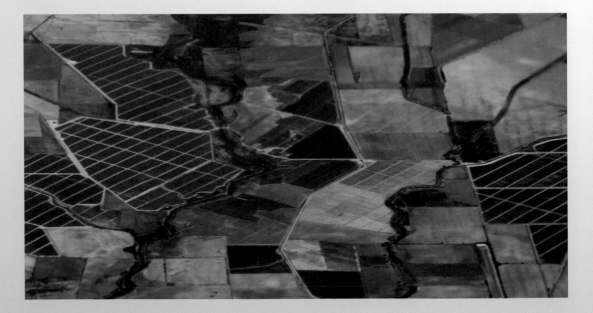

Many parts of the Netherlands lie below sea level. In order to prevent these areas from flooding, large dikes are built in coastal regions creating large areas of reclaimed land called *polders*.

colonial power – a nation (usually European) that controls all the resources of a dependent territory or people, often in a distant part of the world

colony – a group of people who settle in a land distant from their homeland but retain close economic and cultural links with it; the territory they inhabit and control

commerce – trading between nations and individuals

commission – a group of people authorized or directed to carry out a duty or task

communist – one who follows a system of government in which a single authoritarian party controls state-owned means of production

cultivated – prepared or used for growing crops

depiction – a picture, description, or another representation of something

dikes – long ridges of earth constructed along rivers and the seashore to prevent flooding

Dutch East Indies – the islands of Southeast Asia, now the independent state of Indonesia, that came under the control of the Dutch East India Company in the 17th and 18th centuries and remained a Dutch *colony* until 1945. They included the Spice Islands, as the Moluccas (Maluku today) were then known. They were a valuable source of pepper, nutmeg, and other aromatics highly prized in European cooking.

engraver – one who inscribes a design onto a block, plate, or other surface used for printing

equator – the line around Earth joining places the same distance from both the North and South Poles. It is the line of 0 degrees *latitude*.

estuarial waters (estuary) – the wide part of a river where it meets the sea and becomes tidal; an inlet of the sea

frontage – a piece of land that lies adjacent (as to a street, ocean, or river)

grid plan – a town or city layout in which rectangular blocks of buildings are separated by roads intersecting at right angles

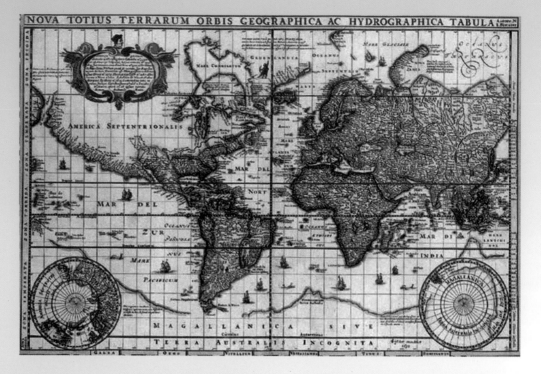

Henry the Navigator (1394–1460) –
the fourth son of King John I of Portugal. He
founded a school for navigators in 1419.
Under his patronage, Portuguese expeditions
ventured out into the Atlantic, discovering
Madeira, the Cape Verde Islands, and the
Azores, and sailed down the west coast of
Africa as far as Sierra Leone.

hunter-gatherers – people who lived by
hunting wild animals and gathering food
from native plants, rather than subsisting by
settled *agriculture*

indigo – a plant that yields a blue vegetable
dye, formerly grown as a plantation crop in
the Caribbean

latitude – a line that joins places of equal
angular distance from the center of Earth in
a north-south direction. The *equator* is at 0
degrees latitude, the poles at 90 degrees
latitude north and south.

longitude – a line connecting places of
equal angular distance from the center of
Earth, measured in degrees east or west of

**The Mercator projection was an
important advance in the science
of cartography. It allowed the
curved surface of Earth to be
represented as a two-dimensional
image without distorting the lines
of latitude and longitude. This
made it ideal for navigators.**

the Prime Meridian, which is at 0 degrees
longitude

manuscript – any hand-written document

map projection – a method of presenting
the curved surface of Earth on a flat piece
of paper or on a computer screen. Different
projections use varying kinds of grid systems
to plot locations.

Mercator projection – a *map
projection* named after its deviser, Gerardus
Mercator (1512–1594), which is commonly
used in making nautical charts. B*earings*
are shown as straight lines on
this projection.

minerals – valuable resources, such as coal, gold, and gas, obtained from within Earth

missionaries – people sent to another country by a church to spread its faith or to do social or medical work

Mughals – a Muslim dynasty that invaded northern India from Central Asia in 1526 and extended its rule throughout the *subcontinent* under a succession of powerful rulers in the 16th and 17th centuries. The arts were cultivated at the Mughal court, and Mughal monuments in India include the Taj Mahal and the Pearl Mosque at Agra.

native peoples – the inhabitants of an area encountered by explorers and colonists. In many cases these people were wiped out or overwhelmed by the colonial power.

navigation – plotting a route and directing a ship, airplane, or other vehicle from one place to another. We now use the word to apply to journeys on foot as well.

New France – an 18th-century term for the area of North America mainly centered around the *estuary* of the St. Lawrence River, but at one time extending to include the whole of the interior, including the Mississippi-Missouri River system, explored and partially colonized by the French

nomads – people whose way of life involves regular, sometime continuous movement. *Hunter-gatherers* travel across wide tracts of country to find food. In many dry parts of the world, pastoral farmers migrate between seasonal pastures with their herds of animals.

nonsensical – having no sense or meaning

paddock – a small field near a house or stable with grazing area for horses

parallels – lines of *latitude*

portolan charts – navigational charts used by European sailors from about 1300 to 1600

Ptolemy – a Greek mathematician and geographer who lived in Alexandria, Egypt, from about 90 to 168 A.D. He was among the first scientists to study and develop *map projections*, and he also wrote textbooks about how to make maps and how to collect information for them. The rediscovery of his works by European scholars in the 15th century stimulated the *Renaissance* study of *cartography*.

relevant – having some bearing on or importance to an issue

Renaissance – a period in European cultural history lasting from the 14th to the 16th century that witnessed an explosion of intellectual activity in the arts and sciences partly as the result of a revival of interest in Classical Greek and Roman culture. The great voyages of discovery owed much to the spirit of the Renaissance and helped spread interest in new ideas about geography and *cartography*.

spices – tasty or aromatic vegetables added to cooked food. Pepper, nutmeg, and cinnamon are examples of eastern spices that were highly prized once encountered in Europe, and for which high prices were paid.

stockade – a tall fence or enclosure made of wooden posts driven into the ground side by side, to keep out enemies or intruders

subcontinent – the large land mass that lies south of the Himalayas; it includes Pakistan, India, and Bangladesh

Land surveying is vital for the creation of accurate maps. The process is still usually performed by surveyors using instruments such as theodolites.

surveying – the measuring of altitudes, angles, and distances on the land surface in order to obtain accurate positions of features that can be mapped. Surveying the oceans and seas also means measuring distances and angles between visible coastal positions, but the third dimension measured is depth rather than height.

telegraph – a method of long-distance communication by coded electric impulses transmitted through wires

terra incognita – literally "unknown land" in Latin; used by cartographers to describe areas of land that they thought existed, but for which there was no proof. The term was also used to describe the unexplored interiors of continents.

terra nullius – literally "empty land" in Latin; used by explorers and colonists who assumed that large parts of the newly discovered world were uninhabited, and therefore could be claimed and settled by incoming people

theodolite – a surveying instrument used to work out the angle between two points on Earth's surface viewed from a third point

title – a document proving that a person owns a piece of land

topographic map – a map that shows natural features such as hills, rivers, and forests, and manmade features such as roads and buildings

United Nations – an organization set up in October 1945 at the end of World War II in order to try to preserve peace and avoid any future wars

Vermeer, Jan (1632–1675) – a Dutch artist who lived in Delft, famous for producing everyday scenes of domestic life that sometimes included prominent maps hung as decoration

watchtower – a high tower in which guards keep watch for the approach of an enemy

Further Reading and Web Sites

Aczel, Amir D. *The Riddle of the Compass: The Invention That Changed the World*. New York: Harcourt, 2001.

Arnold, Caroline. *The Geography Book: Activities for Exploring, Mapping, and Enjoying Your World*. New York: Wiley, 2002.

Barber, Peter, and April Carlucci, eds. *The Lie of the Land*. London: British Library Publications, 2001.

Brown, Carron, ed. *The Best-Ever Book of Exploration*. New York: Kingfisher Books, 2002.

Davis, Graham. *Make Your Own Maps*. New York: Sterling, 2008.

Deboo, Ana. *Mapping the Seas and Skies*. Chicago: Heinemann-Raintree, 2007.

Dickinson, Rachel. *Tools of Navigation: A Kid's Guide to the History & Science of Finding Your Way*. White River Junction, VT: Nomad Press, 2005.

Doak, Robin S. *Christopher Columbus: Explorer of the New World*. Minneapolis, MN: Compass Point Books, 2005.

Ehrenberg, Ralph E. *Mapping the World: An Illustrated History of Cartography*. Washington, D.C.: National Geographic, 2005.

Field, Paula, ed. *The Kingfisher Student Atlas of North America*. Boston: Kingfisher, 2005.

Ganeri, Anita, and Andrea Mills. *Atlas of Exploration*. New York: DK Publishing, 2008.

Graham, Alma, ed. *Discovering Maps*. Maplewood, NJ: Hammond World Atlas Corporation, 2004.

Harvey, Miles. *The Island of Lost Maps: A True Story of Cartographic Crime*. New York: Random House, 2000.

Harwood, Jeremy. *To the Ends of the Earth: 100 Maps That Changed the World*. Newton Abbot, United Kingdom: David and Charles, 2006.

Haywood, John. *Atlas of World History*. New York: Barnes and Noble, 1997.

Hazen, Walter A. *Everyday Life: Exploration & Discovery*. Tuscon, AZ: Good Year Books, 2005.

Henzel, Cynthia Kennedy. *Mapping History*. Edina, MN: Abdo Publishing, 2008.

Jacobs, Frank. *Strange Maps: An Atlas of Cartographic Curiosities*. New York: Viking Studio, 2009.

Keay, John. *The Great Arc: The Dramatic Tale of How India Was Mapped and Everest Was Named*. New York: Harper Collins, 2000.

Levy, Janey. *Mapping America's Westward Expansion: Applying Geographic Tools And Interpreting Maps*. New York: Rosen Publishing, 2005.

Levy, Janey. *The Silk Road: Using a Map Scale to Measure Distances*. New York: PowerKids Press, 2005.

McDonnell, Mark D. *Maps on File*. New York: Facts on File, 2007.

McNeese, Tim. *Christopher Columbus and the Discovery of the Americas*. Philadelphia: Chelsea House, 2006.

Mitchell, Robert, and Donald Prickel. *Contemporary's Number Power: Graphs, Tables, Schedules and Maps*. Lincolnwood, IL: Contemporary Books, 2000.

Oleksy, Walter G. *Mapping the Seas*. New York: Franklin Watts, 2003.

Oleksy, Walter G. *Mapping the Skies*. New York: Franklin Watts, 2003.

Resnick, Abraham. *Maps Tell Stories Too: Geographic Connections to American History*. Bloomington, IN: IUniverse, 2002.

Rirdan, Daniel. *Wide Ranging World Map*. Phoenix, AZ: Exploration, 2002.

Ross, Val. *The Road to There: Mapmakers and Their Stories*. Toronto, Canada: Tundra Books, 2009.

Rumsey, David, and Edith M. Punt. *Cartographica Extraordinaire: The Historical Map Transformed.* Redlands, CA: Esri Press, 2004.

Short, Charles Rennie. *The World through Maps.* Buffalo, NY: Firefly Books, 2003.

Smith, A. G. *Where Am I? The Story of Maps and Navigation.* Toronto, Canada: Fitzhenry and Whiteside, 2001.

Taylor, Barbara. *Looking at Maps.* North Mankato, MN: Franklin Watts, 2007.

Taylor, Barbara. *Maps and Mapping.* New York: Kingfisher, 2002.

Virga, Vincent. *Cartographia: Mapping Civilizations.* London: Little, Brown and Company, 2007.

Wilkinson, Philip. *The World of Exploration.* New York: Kingfisher, 2006.

Wilson, Patrick. *Navigation and Signalling.* Broomall, PA: Mason Crest Publishers, 2002.

Winchester, Simon. *The Map That Changed the World: William Smith and the Birth of Modern Geology.* New York: HarperCollins, 2001.

Zuravicky, Orli. *Map Math: Learning About Latitude and Longitude Using Coordinate Systems.* New York: PowerKids Press, 2005.

Online Resources

www.davidrumsey.com
The David Rumsey map collection. This online library contains around 20,000 historical and modern maps.

http://dma.jrc.it
The mapping collection of the European Commission Joint Research Center. Includes ineractive maps as well as maps documenting environmental and human disasters around the world.

http://etc.usf.edu/Maps/
The University of South Florida's online mapping library. The collection includes historical and modern maps from around the world.

www.lib.utexas.edu/maps
The University of Texas's online map library. The collection includes old CIA maps, historical maps, and thematic maps from around the world.

www2.lib.virginia.edu/exhibits/lewis_clark
An online exhibition at the University of Virginia with information on historic expeditions, including Lewis and Clark.

http://maps.google.com
Google's online mapping resource, includes conventional maps and satellite images for most of the world, as well as street-level photography of Western urban centers.

http://maps.nationalgeographic.com
National Geographic's online mapping service.

http://memory.loc.gov/ammem/gmdhtml/
Map collections from 1500–1999 at the Library of Congress. The collection includes maps made by early explorers, maps of military campaigns, and thematic maps on a variety of topics.

www.nationalatlas.gov
Online national atlas for the United States. Includes customizable topographic maps on a range of different themes.

http://strangemaps.wordpress.com
A frequently updated collection of unusual maps, from maps of imaginary lands to creative ways of displaying data in map form.

www.unc.edu/awmc/mapsforstudents.html
A large collection of free maps, covering many different subjects and regions, hosted by the University of North Carolina.

www.un.org/Depts/Cartographic/
  english/htmain.htm
United Nations mapping agency website. contains maps of the world from 1945 to the present day, including UN maps of conflict areas and disputed territories.

Index

Page numbers written in **boldface** refer to pictures or captions.